PIANO / VOCAL / GUITAR

CHART HITS
2013-2014

ISBN 978-1-4803-8237-4

HAL•LEONARD®
CORPORATION

7777 W. BLUEMOUND RD. P.O. BOX 13819 MILWAUKEE, WI 53213

Visit Hal Leonard Online at
www.halleonard.com

ATLAS

from THE HUNGER GAMES: CATCHING FIRE

Words and Music by GUY BERRYMAN,
JON BUCKLAND, WILL CHAMPION
and CHRIS MARTIN

Car - ry your world.

CUPS
(When I'm Gone)
from the Motion Picture Soundtrack PITCH PERFECT

Words and Music by A.P. CARTER,
LUISA GERSTEIN and HELOISE TUNSTALL-BEHRENS

Moderate Folk

I got my tick-et for the

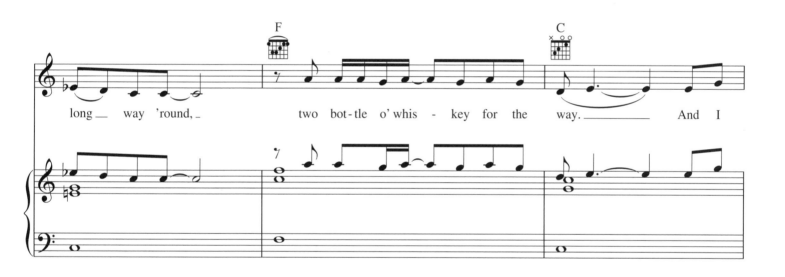

long __ way 'round, __ two bot-tle o' whis - key for the way. _____ And I

sure would like __ some sweet com - pa - ny. __ And I'm leav-in' __ to-mor-row, what do ya

BRAVE

Words and Music by SARA BAREILLES
and JACK ANTONOFF

Moderately

You can be a-maz-in', you can turn a phrase in-to a wea-pon or a drug.

You can be the out-cast or be the back-lash of some-bod-y's lack of love,

or you can start speak-ing up.

COUNTING STARS

Words and Music by
RYAN TEDDER

we'll be count-in' stars. _____ Yeah, we'll be count-in' _____ stars. _____

Moderate Dance groove

I see this

life like a swing-in' vine, _____ swing my heart a-cross the line. _ In my face is flash-in' signs, _

Take that mon-ey, watch it burn. Sink in the riv-er the les - sons I've learned.

Take that mon-ey, watch it burn. Sink in the riv-er the les - sons I've learned.

Take that mon-ey, watch it burn. Sink in the riv-er the les - sons I've learned.

D.S. al Coda

A   F♯m

Ev - 'ry - thing that kills me makes me feel a - live.

DEMONS

Words and Music by DANIEL REYNOLDS,
BENJAMIN McKEE, DANIEL SERMON,
ALEXANDER GRANT and JOSH MOSSER

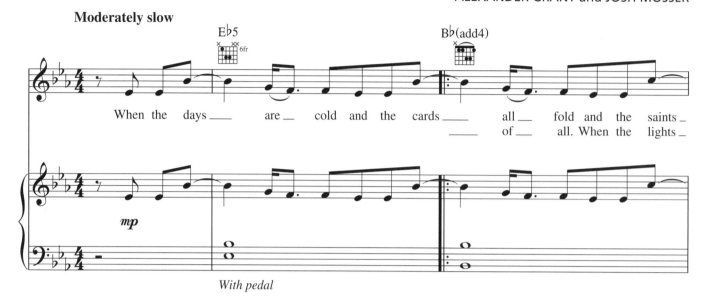

When the days ___ are ___ cold and the cards ___ all ___ fold and the saints ___ ___ of ___ all. When the lights ___

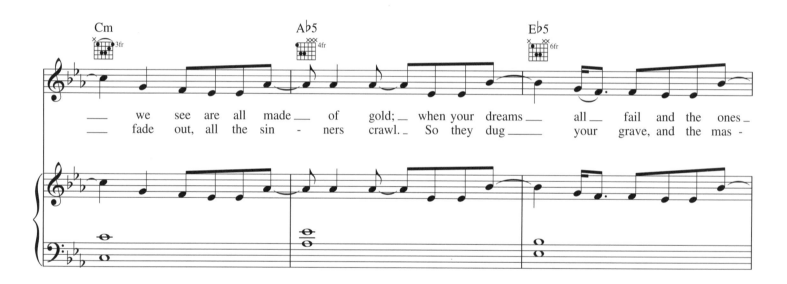

___ we see are all made ___ of gold; when your dreams ___ all ___ fail and the ones ___
___ fade out, all the sin - ners crawl. So they dug ___ your grave, and the mas -

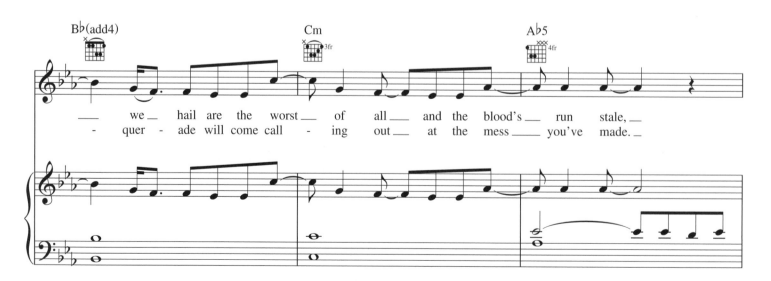

___ we ___ hail are the worst ___ of all and the blood's ___ run stale, ___
- quer - ade will come call - ing out ___ at the mess ___ you've made. ___

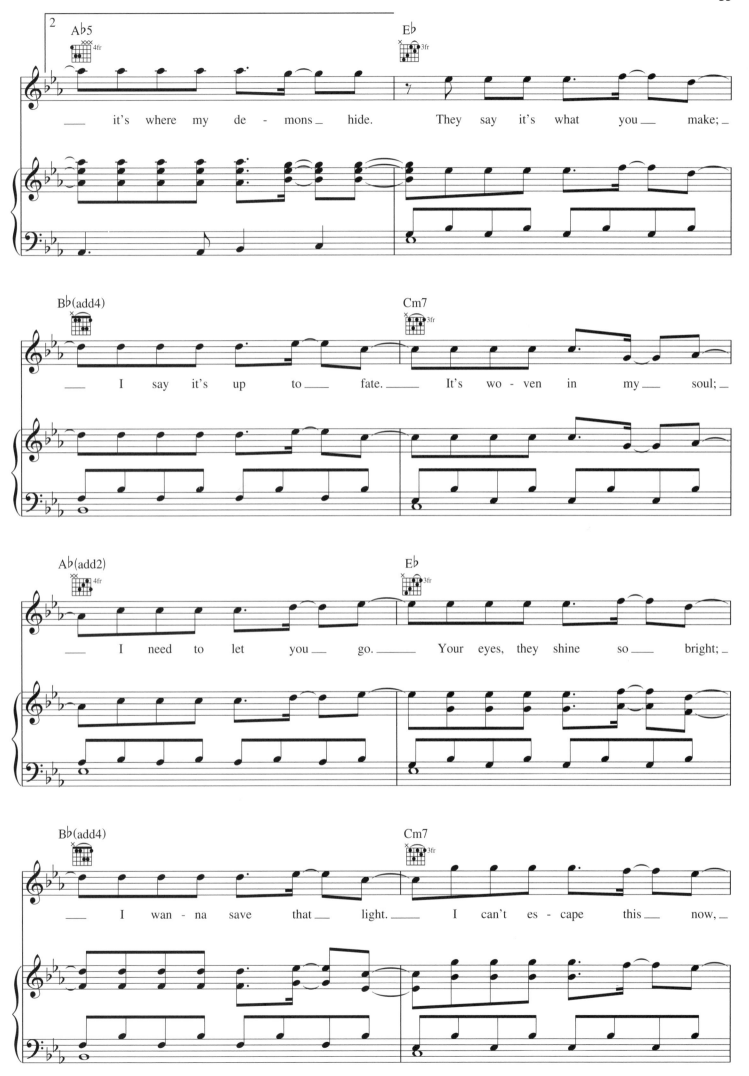

DO WHAT U WANT

Words and Music by STEFANI GERMANOTTA,
PAUL BLAIR, R. KELLY, MARTIN BRESSO
and WILLIAM GRIGAHCINE

Male: Hey, hey, hey, hey, hey, hey, hey.

Hey, hey, hey, hey, hey, hey, hey.

LET HER GO

Words and Music by
MICHAEL DAVID ROSENBERG

And you let her go. ___

Star - ing at the bot - tom of your glass hop - ing one ___ day you'll make a dream
Star - ing at the ceil - ing in the dark, same old emp - ty feel - ing in your

LOVE SOMEBODY

Words and Music by ADAM LEVINE,
NATHANIEL MOTTE, RYAN TEDDER
and NOEL ZANCANELLA

I know your in-sides are feel-ing so hol-low,
You're such a hard act ___ for me to fol-low.

and it's a hard pill for you to swal-
Love me to-day, don't leave me to-mor-

low, yeah.
row, yeah.

But if I

Recorded a half step higher.

ROAR

Words and Music by KATY PERRY,
BONNIE McKEE, MAX MARTIN,
LUKASZ GOTTWALD and HENRY WALTER

ROYALS

Words and Music by JOEL LITTLE
and ELLA YELICH-O'CONNOR

Moderately

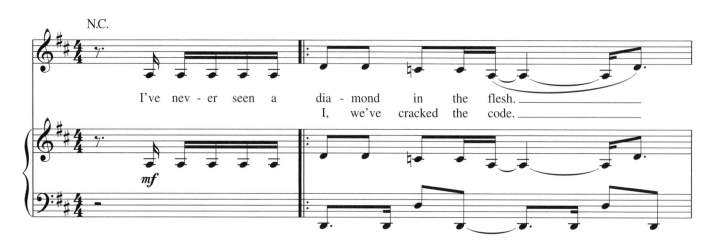

I've nev-er seen a dia-mond in the flesh. _____
I, we've cracked the code. _____

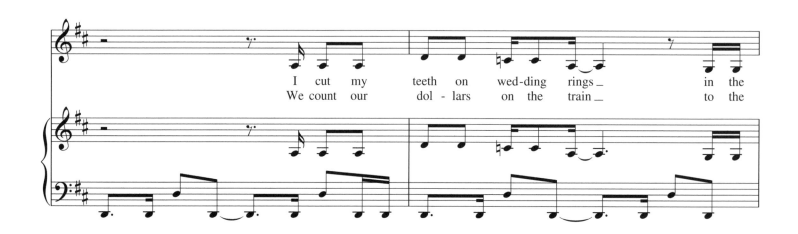

I cut my teeth on wed-ding rings _____ in the
We count our dol-lars on the train _____ to the

mov-ies. _____ And I'm not proud of my ad-dress. _____
par-ty. _____ And ev-'ry-one who knows us knows _____

To Coda

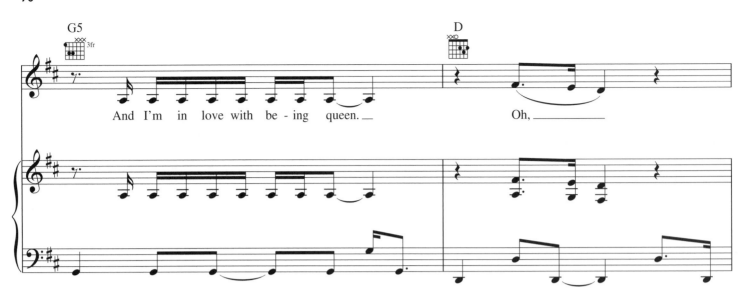

And I'm in love with be - ing queen. ___ Oh, _____

oh, _____ oh, _____ life is game with - out a care. ___ We aren't

caught up in your love af - fair. ___ And we'll nev - er be

Let me live that fan - ta - sy.

SAY SOMETHING

Words and Music by IAN AXEL,
CHAD VACCARINO and MIKE CAMPBELL

SAFE AND SOUND

Words and Music by RYAN TAKACS MERCHANT
and SEBOUH (SEBU) SIMONIAN

STORY OF MY LIFE

Words and Music by JAMIE SCOTT,
JOHN HENRY RYAN, JULIAN BUNETTA,
HARRY STYLES, LIAM PAYNE,
LOUIS TOMLINSON, NIALL HORAN
and ZAIN MALIK

Fast, in a driving 4

Writ-ten in these walls are the sto-ries that I can't ex-plain.

Writ-ten on these walls are the col-ors that I can't change.

I

I

SWEATER WEATHER

Words and Music by JESSE RUTHERFORD,
ZACHARY ABELS and JEREMY FREEDMAN

WAKE ME UP!

Words and Music by TIM BERGLING,
ALOE BLACC and MICHAEL EINZIGER

To Coda

time   I was find - in' __ my - self _____ {and I _____
                                              {and I, _____   did - n't know   I ____ was

lost. _____

CODA

I did-n't know_ I ____ was lost. ____

Lead vocal ad lib.

End vocal ad lib.

UNCONDITIONALLY

Words and Music by KATY PERRY,
MAX MARTIN, LUKASZ GOTTWALD
and HENRY WALTER